First Facts

Earn It, Save It, Spend It!

Earn Money

by Emily Raij

PEBBLE
a capstone imprint

First Facts are published by Pebble
1710 Roe Crest Drive, North Mankato, Minnesota 56003
www.mycapstone.com

Library of Congress Cataloging-in-Publication Data
Names: Raij, Emily, author.
Title: Earn money / by Emily Raij.
Description: North Mankato, Minnesota : Pebble, [2020] | Series: First facts.
 Earn it, save it, spend it! | Includes index.
Identifiers: LCCN 2018060560| ISBN 9781977108319 (hardcover) | ISBN
 9781977110022 (pbk.) | ISBN 9781977108517 (ebook pdf)
Subjects: LCSH: Money--Juvenile literature. | Occupations--Juvenile
 literature. | Wages--Juvenile literature.
Classification: LCC HG221.5 .R353 2020 | DDC 331.2/1--dc23
LC record available at https://lccn.loc.gov/2018060560

Editorial Credits
Karen Aleo, editor; Sarah Bennett, designer; Tracy Cummins, media researcher;
Kathy McColley, production specialist

Photo Credits
Capstone Studio: Karon Dubke, Back Cover, Design Element; iStockphoto:
ljubaphoto, 13; Shutterstock: Andrey_Popov, 7, ANURAK PONGPATIMET, 21,
baibaz, 5, DedMityay, 9, Dragon Images, 15, Maria Evseyeva, 17, Monkey Business
Images, 11, Nik Merkulov, Design Element, oliveromg, 19, Thomas J. Sebourn, Cover

All internet sites appearing in back matter were available and accurate when this book was sent to press.

Printed and bound in China.
1671

Table of Contents

Why Do People Earn Money?

Money is important to pay for things. People earn, or make, money to buy the things they need. Needs are food, housing, and clothing. Not everything people buy is a need. Sometimes people buy things they would like to have.

When people earn money for work, they receive a paycheck. They have to make decisions about what to do with their paychecks. People can spend, save, or **donate** money. It's important for people to make good decisions with their money. They must be able to save to buy what they need.

FACT

Once money is spent, that money is not available anymore. Money will then have to be earned and saved.

donate—to give something as a gift to a charity or cause

People can keep money in a savings account at the bank. They can **deposit** money into the bank account or **withdraw** money from the account.

Loans

Sometimes people do not have the money to make a big purchase, such as a car. Banks can provide **loans**. Loans are money given to someone to make a purchase. Loans are paid back to the bank by the person who borrowed the money.

deposit—to put money into a bank account

withdraw—to take money out of a bank account

loan—money that is borrowed with a plan to pay it back

budget—a plan for spending money

8

Many people create a plan for saving and spending money. This is called a **budget**. A budget shows how much money can be earned, spent, and saved.

CHAPTER 2

Ways to Earn Money

How do people earn money for the things they need and want? They work at a job! There are all kinds of jobs. Some people sell **goods** at stores. Some of the money made by selling goods goes into the **employees'** paychecks.

FACT

Companies make money by selling goods for more than they cost to make. This money is called **profit**.

goods—things that can be bought or sold

employee—a worker hired and paid by a company

profit—the money that a business makes after expenses have been paid

Other people provide **services**.
A service is work that helps others.
Teachers, doctors, and car mechanics
provide services. They get paid for
the service.

On the Job

Different skills and knowledge are needed for
different jobs. Some people go to college to learn
these skills. Others receive training at their job.
Doctors go to college and medical school. Then
they complete their training in a hospital.

service—work that helps others, such as providing medical
care, fixing cars, or cutting hair

Some people start their own businesses. They make and sell goods or provide services.

Companies pay employees **income**. Many companies put this payment into the employees' bank accounts. Employees can use this money at any time. Some workers are paid with a paper check they deposit into their bank account. Income can also be cash. These dollars and coins are the **currency** people use to buy things.

income—money earned for work done

currency—the type of money a country uses

CHAPTER 3

Try It!

Think of a service you can provide. There are lots of ways you can earn money in your neighborhood. And you can help neighbors at the same time! Ask neighbors if they need help with chores. Lots of little jobs can turn into steady income.

FACT
Neighbors often need help walking their dogs, raking leaves, or washing their cars.

Selling goods is another way to make money. You can make crafts, such as jewelry or artwork. With an adult's help, have a yard sale to sell these crafts. You can sell things you no longer use too. Post signs with the date, time, and place of your sale.

What are the reasons you want to earn money? Make a list of goals, such as buying a new book. Then figure out how long it will take to earn the money. As you earn money, save it until you have enough to meet your goal. You have to save to spend!

Glossary

budget (BUH-juht)—a plan for spending money

currency (KUR-uhn-see)—the type of money a country uses

deposit (di-PAH-zuht)—to put money into a bank account

donate (DOH-nayt)—to give something as a gift to a charity or cause

employee (im-PLOY-ee)—a worker hired and paid by a company

goods (GUDZ)—things that can be bought or sold

income (IN-kuhm)—money earned for work done

loan (LOHN)—money that is borrowed with a plan to pay it back

profit (PROF-it)—the money that a business makes after expenses have been paid

service (SUR-viss)—work that helps others, such as providing medical care, fixing cars, or cutting hair

withdraw (with-DRAW)—to take money out of a bank account

Read More

Eagen, Rachel. *Learning About Earning.* Money Sense: An Introduction to Financial Literacy. New York: Crabtree Publishing Company, 2017.

Schuh, Mari. *Earning Money.* Money Matters. Minneapolis: Bellwether Media, 2016.

Sherman, Jill. *Money: What You Need to Know. Fact Files.* North Mankato, MN: Capstone, 2017.

Internet Sites

Practical Money Skills: Peter Pig's Money Counter
http://www.practicalmoneyskills.com/play/peter_pigs_money_counter#

The Mint: How Banks Work
http://www.themint.org/kids/how-banks-work.html

Critical Thinking Questions

1. What are some ways people earn money? How can you earn money?

2. What are some reasons people earn money?

3. Should people spend all their money right away? Why or why not?

Index